Little Hugs

Encouragement
for your soul

◆ FriesenPress

Suite 300 - 990 Fort St
Victoria, BC, V8V 3K2
Canada

www.friesenpress.com

ISBN
978-1-5255-5357-8 (Hardcover)
978-1-5255-5358-5 (Paperback)
978-1-5255-5359-2 (eBook)

1. POETRY, INSPIRATION & RELIGIOUS

Distributed to the trade by The Ingram Book Company

Little Hugs

Encouragement
for your soul

RAMAN MANDER

This book is dedicated to all those souls
in need of a hug.

This is for you.

You are beautiful.

You are so much more than the world sees of you.

I want you to hold me close to your heart.

Take me with you.

I want to be there when you need love the most.

Take me when your delicate heart needs a hug.

Use me.

You deserve all the little hugs in the world.

Hugs for your loving soul.

I would like to thank my mom and
my dad, my other half, my family, and
my friends for the encouragement
and support during the creation
of this collection. Grateful for the
numerous little hugs that I received
throughout this.

RELEASING

My heart is so full

That your love is overflowing into my arteries,

Into my veins.

Your love ceases to pull

Pull me back, *backwards.*

Only to meet with you

In my heart,

Where it is so full.

Overflowing

With you,

God.

Abundance

Get back to your centre—
That gravitational pull
Weighing you down.
Like the earth's magnetic field
That holds tiny humans
So close to its surface.
Hugging our feet,
Pulling us down
Individually
To our own centre.
Just as you pull yourself down
To your heart,
Bring yourself back to your centre.

Alignment

One-faced moon,

You create so much commotion.

The tides are heavily impacted

By you.

Wave after wave—

You have great influence.

You burn like the sun, yet without any fire.

Shining so bright, even in darkness,

Always rotating with me.

We both go through cycles.

Yours are more consistent.

Call me two-faced,

Won't ya?

Wildfire

You can't touch the smell of lavender in her perfume.

You can't hear the egg fusing with sperm.

You can't taste the words of anger from injustice.

You can't smell teardrops falling on the sides of their cheeks.

You can't see a broken heart—ache

With so much weight.

But you can fall in love

Without falling

On your knees.

Yes.

My heart feels heavy.

My senses are out of control. Redirecting,

Hoping they find their purpose.

Hoping I find my purpose.

A c h e

How did God make the earth so still
That we do not shake
When it rotates?
That we spin in circles
Without getting dizzy
And falling on our faces?
So still, yet we keep moving.

Balance

Everlasting —

You are the diamonds that fall on Saturn.

Forever and always,

You will remain.

Eternal

An unborn child has no religion
Until we give it one.
I tell you that an unborn child has no religion,
Yet we take away its nonexistent religion.
We proclaim ourselves the greater good.
We *categorize* that unborn child into a religion.
I tell you that an unborn child has no religion,
Yet we create a decision at its first breath.
I tell you that unborn child has no religion,
For its only religion is humanity.

Compartmentalization

Your energy is yours.
Do not let anyone take that away.
How dare you let them enter your bubble?

Pop, pop, pop

Do you get frustrated
When you are hurt?
All you ever gave was
Your mind, body, and soul.
That was all you gave.

Donation

I apologize for the way
I soak in your radiating glow.
I crave your physical existence
Consistently.
Forgive me
For my obsession
With your divine spirit,
Which continuously tickles my soul.
I blame me, too.
For reacting in giggles,
For acting like your lover.
I feel helpless all the time.
I give you control
Because I would fall and fall
Before I tried to lift a finger.
- sorry for what?

Amusement

There is magic
In all the humans
You encounter.
Not all of them show you
Their magic tricks.

Illusion

Separate yourself.
You and your self
Becoming one.
Why so much chaos, my love?
Chaos.

You define yourself by chaos.
I said
Separate yourself
From chaos,
For chaos is not your name.

Disconnected

Today, I stood up for myself

For myself.

I said no to temptation

So I could heal.

I said no to anger

That rushed in my blood.

I said no to the thoughts

That pinched my insides

So I could feel.

I said yes to the universe.

For it was real.

I stood up.

Determined

My insides feel funny
With a longing for you.
I am nervous,
Doing all I can to keep myself occupied.
It is not that I do not trust you.
I hope your heart never changes its mind.
You are the best thing
that has ever happened to me.

Pause

You feel handfuls of ache
From the slightest
Inconvenience for others.
You tear up
When voices are raised
Because the sounds are loud enough
To cause treble in your heart.
But why close off
All the love you give to the world
In handfuls —
When you yourself are an example
Of a sensitive heart?
You need you
More than you know.

Delicate

Little highs.
My heart flutters.
I am seeking a high.
It is quarter past three.
The moon is out
And I have the itches.

Adventure

I have no words
To describe
How I feel.

Reality

My heart hurts
From all the ache you gave me.
I would be lying if I denied any pain.

Discomfort

Noise.

Loud and echoing

Inside my mind.

My soul quivers

At your movement.

Creeping inside my body.

Shaking me constantly.

Consistent feedback

Screaming at me!

Listen to your own voice.

You have lost yourself

In others.

Distraction

Dear soul,

Why do you get so uneasy?

O, how you quiver

When you hear noises.

Your startle reflex

Shakes.

Bolts.

Dear soul,

Why do you quiver?

You know the universe is hugging you.

There is no room for movement.

O soul, God hugs you O so tight.

Jittery

I have so much love for you, God.
There is

NO SPACE

In my body
To contain it.

Embodiment

Slowly
I let God into my life.
Quickly
He let me into mine.

Home

Soul craving.

Mind taking.

Body aching.

I

Am

Passionate

About

You.

Longing

They reached out
To extend their arms to you.
But not all arms
Are in arms' reach of you.

Distance

The lightning bolt

On my wrist

Strikes me.

When I catch sight of it

Fierce it reads.

That is what I am

Or tell myself.

I have many insecurities

Within me,

Internal fears that haunt me.

<u>I am</u> my own demon.

Flesh composing of maggots.

Hoping they will transform into butterflies

That will help me escape

Myself.

Transformation

I, too, have felt senseless.
For being sucked into a *tornado*
Then coming out **alive**.

Gasping

Along the way
We will find each other.
A little more mature,
A little more developed,
A little more open-hearted,
A little more closed off,
A little more..

Sprouted

If you keep
picking
and
picking at it,
Eventually it will fall.
If you keep
picking
and picking at me,
I will fall.

Wilt

I set aside what was left behind.

I never asked you, I never bothered.

What was there to lose?

Perhaps, it was too much to capture.

I walked.

I followed your side.

Hand on hand.

One path— was it the same path?

Moments worth of work.

Was everything much more beautiful,

More beautiful than when you first looked through?

Left with no words, should I even bother?

Did you ask for the world? How so…

Could you possibly grasp onto what was never yours?

For better or worse.

More pure, more evil.

Let you take over the world.

I couldn't

And I wouldn't,

I could have only given you what was mine

Because what was mine, was yours.

You couldn't possibly know, could you?

What is left now?

Life.

Memories.

Memories that are loose, with nothing captured

Leaving behind what is left of my cold laughs.

My breath remains numb, for I do not feel.

Do you see the light?

Light in my powerhouse.

It beats, it beats,

It beats a thousand words.

This world keeps getting painful

For that,

My walls keep shutting in.

Faster

She screams in agony!
Labouring in pain
As the umbilical cord clamps her unborn.
She becomes her own.
To each, their own.
Only to pass on her mother's cry.

Surviving

Dear God,

You created me.

My eyes.

My ears.

My mouth.

You gave me body parts of strength

And weakness.

I bet you are probably giggling inside me.

That is why my hearts beating faster

And faster and *faster*.

Use me. Ignite me.

Light the fire in me.

My arms are reaching out.

Hug me back, I insist.

When I do embrace your presence

The little joyful child in me moves.

A picture that makes me smile.

I am getting high off you—

Little did I know your giggles are contagious.

Endemic

From you, I feel so far.

Like the earth never once saw sun

And a single seed never reached its true form.

As I hear the train whistle in complete darkness,

I understand now.

This is how a dark soul must feel.

An empty, passionless human.

Zoned out, glaring through the glass window.

I shook my head into clarity

Only to catch myself glaring into my own eyes.

Potential

Love says

Do not try to go on

Without me.

I am the sole purpose

Behind everything.

I am in a room with two lovers

Embracing each other.

I am outside

Where the sun rays bring your face to a glow.

Leaving behind a radiating smile.

Yes.

I am the reason

You are also in tears

From words that hurt your loving soul.

From actions that put your world at a halt.

You see,

I have to go through you

For you to

See me,

Take me,

Use me,

And
Appreciate me.

Shine

You keep
Ignoring the lighter
Only to have it flickering.
Flicker, Flicker—
To notice there is no fuel in the lighter,
Until one spark
Lights your fire.

Twinkle

The moon is awake at night.

Though it never ceases to complain—

So am I,

Awake,

Sleepless,

And

Complaining..

Restless

I think I feel a wave coming

At me.

Stroking my cheek

To let me know

It does not stop here.

Bigger waves are coming

With moonlight.

Smaller waves have set themselves aside.

Unknown

My driving force is God,
Taking the steering wheel
So I can enjoy the ride.

Control

I am lost and trying to be found.
My hearts transmitter is running,
Running, and running
On low-battery mode.
It sends signals to the universe,
Hoping to receive a signal back.
I am feeling exhausted
But I keep recharging myself.
I wake up
And hope today is the day
The signal will hold my charge.

Surge

Learning to find
Hearts with love.
Embracing yourself
Without any judgement
Or expectation
That you be
A certain way.

Expectations

You focus on the future.

How you want to be.

How you believe you need to be.

Spitting words like you are supposed to be

A being of love.

Love is through actions.

Words alone do not phantom

The electrifying energy

Love gives.

You justify

Love through words.

Throwing words,

Which will bring

Settlement to the discussion.

You are a being of peace,

My child.

Others hurt too.

Impaired

You are the name of the light

of the night.

You are the source of the power

of the universe.

You are the whole of the fumes

that I inhale.

You are light.

Light of God.

That is my name.

Ramandeep

I am a being of love.

I am a being of peace.

I am a being of being grateful

For all the love that I receive.

For all the love that I give,

Only to have it come back to me.

I crave universal love.

One where there are no expectations.

No ache.

No pain.

I put up these walls

Because those expectations are increasing.

Walls of universal love are evolving.

Cycling

I open up with so much courage.
You shut me down with so much ego.

Torpedo

I keep giving,

Giving,

Giving,

Giving,

Giving,

Giving,

Giving,

Giving,

Giving,

But I can't help myself.

Reciprocate

BLESS ALL THOSE BROKEN SOULS WHO LOOKED
FOR LIGHT
But got **darkness**.

Illuminate

I find myself
Only to save myself
From you.

Hiding

We all are always evolving and changing

Like seasons.

The core of who we are

will always be rooted in our soul.

Origin

God is the wildest kisser.

Kissing our souls—

MUAH!

Caress

Dear soul,

How do you contemplate

To be passionate

Or engulfed?

Their tiny lengthy hands

Reach in

But never grasp

What could be held.

Liberate

Congratulations!
It's a boy!
It's a girl!
Call me a hopeless romantic.
Will they never say
It's a healthy baby!

Conditioned

Dear universe,

How many moments do we live?

Why do you let us manipulate your picture?

With strong associations—

We use you.

Take away your resources.

We forget, continuously,

That prayer fuels the earth.

Materials are materials.

Energy

Inside us

We have a flame burning with God.

During highs and lows

It gets brighter or dimmer.

Imagine strangers adding oil to the flame

When it is already burning at its finest.

Who are they to put that oil in you?

Who are they to fire your fire?

Transparency

I move on
To find a place
Where I am content
As a being.

Fulfillment

I feel overwhelmed
Thinking of doing so much
With a list that keeps growing.
I get frustrated at myself
Because I cannot say no.
I feel like I am not superwoman.

Limitations

Dear turbulence,

I fear you may startle me.

I shake at the thought of shaking.

Not knowing when you will arrive.

Be nice when you visit.

Hold onto me,

Won't you?

Disturbance

Heart racing.

Leg shaking.

Eyes gazing.

I am *trying* to stay distracted.

Symptoms

We all want something priceless.

How about a smile

With no favours returned?

Rare

This time was different.

It was me.

I was different.

I held onto God's arm.

Backbone

I am in another country,
Yet I keep thinking about you.

Focus

I picture you in control.
Take me as I am,
For you water my soul.

Surrender

Leaves me wondering
If I am becoming
More
Sensitive
Or aware
Or open minded
Or plain crazy???

Questionable

I cannot help but feel
As if I owe others an explanation.
When I try to justify
How wrong you treat me,
You refuse to listen.
You shut the door
Before I have the chance to knock.
I hope you come to know
My soul hurts, too.

Voice

I do not get angry.

Rarely.

If anything, I get angry at myself

For being angry.

I try to be kind to my own soul.

Rarely.

Gentle

I get hurt
Because all the ache in the world
Feels like a punch in the chest.

Shattered

Why, my child,
Do you need validation
From the outside world
When I declare my love for you?

Consent

Without you,
I would still be searching
For you.
Wondering if
God made me a soulmate,
Only to let us lovers
Bump into each other
Like flies—
Always on the go.

Collision

Give me back the key

To empathy

So I feel sensitive again

To all the world's aches

It has given me.

I chose to be numb

But now I cannot enjoy happy times.

Desensitized

Some guy
Gave me a teddy
That was holding a clothed heart.
The heart separated,
Leaving it dangling from one paw.
That guy took a fine needle
And pinned the heart together.
Little did he know
My guy would pin our hearts together.

Union

You bring forward

passion

and

love

in

me.

How can I not write about you

When I think about you?

Affection

Pray for the souls aching on a full moon.

Celestial

Rain.

Sunshine.

Lightning.

Rainbow.

God painted a picture for me today.

There was one yesterday, I bet.

I was too busy

To notice.

Present

You leave the light on
To see through my soul.
It brings you ease
To remove the dark core
Of my coconut heart.
Once it pours out emotions,
A single fracture gives
You and I transparency
For my soul.

Defense

Less seeking love from others,
More seeking for love from God.
Stop being *in* love.
Start <u>being</u> love.

Love

Throbbing heart—
Aching like post-surgery.
Why do you hurt?
Why do you feel so much hurt?

Misery

My soul weighs a thousand pounds.

Even I cannot carry it,

For it feels as heavy

As brick

And as light as a feather.

Burden

Shift your gaze
Towards a full moon.
Only then you will come to know
It is crying
For help.

Sorrow

Cannot wait for your birth
So you can unconditionally LOVE me, child.

Unlimited

I look back

To a time and place

I felt hurt.

Thinking I would never survive.

Here I am.

Hurt again.

Surviving.

Capable

Instead of avoiding me—
Look me in the eyes.

Confrontation

I returned
To a place of healing.
When I look into the outer layer of my heart,
All I see is
More layers peeling off.
I am letting light in
So healing can begin.

Renewal

I feel as if I give

And give

Pieces of myself.

When in reality,

I am one quantity

Trying to break myself

To give care and love to you.

I continuously get hurt

Trying to break myself

When I do not need to.

Broken

If God did not give you tears,

How would you reach inside those wet eyes

To notice that each of them carry an ocean?

For only you can feel

Tears down your cheeks,

And circumstances can see them.

Emotions

Soul deep.
It hurts in places
I never knew existed in me.
Your love will suffice.

Enough

There is a time

Where you will stand

In the middle of a storm

Moving right through you.

Whirling around you

As you try to move through it.

You use your hands to push through,

Only to have it push back at you.

There is no escape.

You are stuck

In this whirlwind of a storm.

You are frozen now.

You can only hope that the storm will pass

And you will be free.

Independence

Trying to understand someone who is not present in your life

Is like trying to understand—

Is like trying

To

Understand

Someone

Who

Is

Not

Present

In

Your

Life.

Past

You only get hurt if you have expectations.
You only get hurt if you are embarrassed.
You only get hurt if you are hurting.
You only get hurt
Because IT HURT AND HURTS.

Intentions

Picture your soul.

What flows out of it?

Is it negative energy

Or are you blooming flowers?

Unfolding

You are so cold

That when someone takes a step towards you,

You take a step back

So their energy does not reflect onto you.

Guard

My heart aches
Like a hammer striking a bird.
It hurts like a bitch.
I tell you it hurts.
You knew I was a delicate rose,
Yet you took off each petal
And enjoyed it.

Throbbing

Even our loved ones

Seem cold

Because they pick and choose

Their loved ones.

Selective

You crave love

That does not want you.

In all forms,

You feel unwanted.

Billions of souls,

Yet you manufacture your own.

Wanted

You know their intentions.
You choose to reach out
And become tangled
In puppet strings.

Knots

If God is a drug,
Then I am addicted.

Appetite

You create a barricade
For all those
Who hurt you.

Shield

Ignite my flesh.

I continuously blamed myself

For hurting others when I was told

That they do not appreciate my consoling,

My comfort,

My hugs,

And

My love.

Now I blame myself for not seeing

That they were tearing me apart

By refusing

To let me be me.

Flames

With the lack of knowledge I had at 11 years old,

I tried to colour my own face

Using shades of brown

To blend in the fine line

Between brown and beige.

Cutting my hair

So my bangs fall

On the discoloured side of my face.

Continuously having eyes stare at me

Like I am extraterrestrial.

Being asked if I was burned as a child

Or had hot tea spill on my face.

Being told numerously

That my makeup was not blended in

Properly

When my face was clean.

Questions on questions.

Asking my mother and father

For answers

So I could give responses

The next time I was asked.

The tears were not enough

To cover my face.

Seeking for answers
From the medical profession,
Hoping they could cure me.
Frustration building up
Because there was no cure.
No equipment could fix me.
Endless questions and remarks.
At 25, I come to love me.
My face holds a mark so deep,
It marks a new birth in me.

Birthmark

Ever feel so empty
That you look up
To find that
Nothing can comfort you?
Emptiness.
It is so deep—
Even you cannot find the end.

Hollow

My arms are spread wide,
Knowing God is my parachute
Through the adrenaline and unknown.

Faith

My heart feels heavy today.

Pain

Then you learn
You cannot be at two places at once.
You get exhausted trying to be superwoman.
Always saving souls.
When will you save your own?

Rescue

God sends

Beautiful souls

To encourage me.

Beautiful souls send

Powerful words

To encourage you.

Powerful words send

Small messages

To encourage others.

Small messages send

Positive vibes

To encourage encouragers.

Positive vibes send

My heart into hibernation.

I cannot contain my excitement

Over beautiful souls.

God sent.

Sending...

Connected

If you were numb before,
Do not paralyze yourself now.

Spirit

I feel like I have all this hurt
from people.
Hurt is given in a bottle
That is put in my hand by others.
I am afraid.
If I hold it tight,
It will break in my hand
And the glass will cut me.
Now I refuse to hold the bottle.
I find flowers to hold instead.

Awareness

There was a knot in my tummy.

It hurt.

Tighter and tighter it got.

I felt like I was giving

Not only to you,

But others as well.

I forgot about myself,

As always.

Once again,

God looks in awe.

God questions me—

I am giving you so much LOVE, my child.

Why is that not enough for you?

Supply

Are you anxious

Because you are

In your own head?

Receiving the clarity

You asked for is not enough.

You do not have room

To juggle your brain.

Are you anxious

Because this space

Allows for you to plan

The future?

You give yourself the creeps.

Why are you anxious?

Frazzled

The more time I spend with myself,

The more time I have for clarity

To seek you.

The more time I give to people,

The more I find you.

Clarity

Giving love
Where it is being revealed.
Revealing love
Where it is being given.

Mutual

Show me where love is being given,
So I can appreciate it with all my heart.

Gratitude

There came a time where I became so negative

That I felt trapped.

I felt as if I was an attic

With an awful stench.

I was that expired can of food

Tucked underneath boxes,

Knowing I would be used

As a last resort.

I understood you needed me

But not until you needed me.

I was one of the many dying flowers

When Autumn took its course.

Unfortunately,

Spring never hit me.

Nor did I care enough to let light touch me

Because where I came from

There was no room for change.

There was no room for understanding,

Because

My expiry date was 17 years ago.

There came a time

Where I was so negative

That I made myself feel trapped.

Seasons

Today
I took a breath towards freedom.
I can feel my face glowing.
Embracing all the positive energy
That is flowing
Within me.
Grateful, I am,
For putting aside
What is unhealthy for me.

Discipline

Have you ever
Looked into the eyes of a child
To feel innocence
Staring right through you?

Transparency

Living out love

Is like asking

Why there is an elephant in the room?

Seriously,

WHO PUT THE ELEPHANT IN THE ROOM?

It is about the person who took the energy

To put the elephant in the room.

The thought process.

The creativity.

The state of mind

To give into

Such an action.

Being love

Is not a checklist, dear.

It is not by words that show action

But actions that live up to words.

Being in love, loves love.

And

Puts love in the room.

Imagination

A part of me

Learns to let go

A part of you.

One piece at a time,

I dig in deep

Into private places

To find that my own dark past

Haunts me.

Secrets

Sometimes I go to a place

So deep in my soul

That my heart hurts.

Heavier

And

Heavier it gets.

Escape

My mind wanders off to a place

That overwhelms me.

It scares me because of the places it takes me.

I take myself on a journey

To trembling waters,

Finding myself drowning

In *what ifs*.

Thinking

You have been caged.

Restricted to your internal desires.

Only seeing limitations.

You find yourself stuck.

You see horizontal lines at an armpit distance.

You stay still.

You make some noise

When you are in need.

You claw.

You bite.

You pick and pick

At what you have.

If you were set free,

Would you have the survival skills to protect yourself?

To ensure your own safety?

To ensure that bigger predators will not cage you?

To ensure that you can be your own protector?

Will you stay still

Or will you make noise

When you are free?

Bang!

I grew up wanting a tattoo of the word *believe*.

I grew up wanting a tattoo of the word **believe**.

I grew up wanting a tattoo of the word <u>believe</u>.

To remind myself to believe

To be in constant reminder of you

I grew up—

I now believe.

Perspective

Align your words and actions.
Ostentatious living
Empties your pockets.
Leaving behind [nothing]

Meaningless

Feeling overwhelmed
By where to start.
My heart vibrates
At endless callings.

Mission

Fingerprints and tree-trunk lines
Are beautifully created.
Continuous circles
Meeting
Endless points.
Trees matter. You matter.
Matter matters.

Infinitely

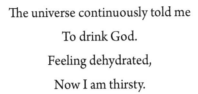

The universe continuously told me
To drink God.
Feeling dehydrated,
Now I am thirsty.

Swallow

This one is for all the moments
That you have held back your tears.
Felt your glossy eyes
Stare down and look away.
Swallowing your own saliva.
Trying not to let out a quivery sound
As you are biting your bottom lip.
Your throat is tightening up
And you are forgetting to **exhale**.
You try to brush off your emotions.
Hoping when you are alone,
You can release
By yourself.

Pause

Ever process sitting in a plane?

Flying into clouds.

Having your feet touch the ground, per se.

The thin piece of metal

Between you and the ground

Is a vast amount of space

That underlines your faith.

I picture God

Holding the plane

Between his thumb and index finger,

Yelling "weeeeeeee!"

You and I are going on an adventure!

Reassurance

Bestest friend.

We had a fallout.

Fingers were pointed.

Words were said.

Some hurtful than others.

I still hold you

Close to my heart

Despite the ultimatum you gave me.

I love the good in you, *still.*

Hear about accomplished dreams

You once shared with me

Coming to life.

Secretly applauding for you,

Hoping the waves that come with each clap

Send enough vibrations for you to know

It is from me.

You let me go

So I could grow.

You let me go

So you could grow.

You let us go

So we could grow, separately.

How selfish would it have been

For you to consume me

And

For me to consume you?

How little the world would see of a blossoming you.

Cheering

I wonder

If our "ship" was real.

I truly enjoyed our sail.

The waves run through my mind

To think I found a friend

That genuinely cared

About the way

The stars align.

To see the brightest star

Pointing north

So we always find each other

When we are lost.

We were always going towards the same direction.

Now we intentionally get lost—

Having hope that we do not end up in the same direction.

We used to talk.

Shipwreck

You told me
We have fallouts because people change.
Yet you and I changed
Because we had a fallout.

Absent

I feel as if
All the hurt I have received from the world
Is forgotten when you are in me.
Your love not only makes up for it,
But it overflows.

Pouring

My stomach is in a tight knot.

I feel scared.

Trusting that my reach for God

Is strong enough to untie the knot

That is hurting me.

Making me feel

Nothing

But

Hollow

And

Empty.

Echo

Dear human,

I am kind of upset too.

You call your mind foolish.

All I see is a curious mind searching for me.

You are worthy, child.

A worthy child.

How could I forget you?

All you saw was darkness for 9 months

Until this exact day.

Until your blind blue eyes saw light for the first time.

Now that you have seen light,

Why are you so afraid to step in the darkness?

I am working on you.

I want you to fall so hard

And keep on falling,

Knowing

I will be there to catch you.

Love, the wax on that flame inside you.

Ignite

Life is simple.

You and I are complex.

Life can be complex.

You and I can be simple.

Relationships

I want nothing

But love

For you and I.

Nothing but love

For you and I.

To be love in the world.

To not pick

And choose

And wait

For the other to hurt the other.

That would be the opposite.

Do you want nothing?

Wishing

Human.

You are evolving, growing, and changing in numerous ways.

Keep flowing and glowing.

Embrace who you are now.

Embrace who you are becoming.

Recognize who you are right now.

Recognize who you are becoming.

Who are you?

Little progresses mean big impact.

We may perceive ourselves as an image

We have for ourselves in the future.

Outside of that, who are you right now?

Why do those components make who you are?

How incredible is it that those components make such a

beautiful you?

Bleeding

You came into this world crying.

Having your chest rise.

Sucking air in.

Filling those little alveoli with oxygen.

Letting all the fluid in your lungs release

So you could release your mother from working

And you could stop exhausting her

Of her oxygen.

Now you are crying for help

Because your mother is taking longer to feed you.

You are too little to understand that

She cannot afford formula.

She cannot afford time to feed you.

She cannot afford you.

You learn that malnutrition is your friend.

Deprived

Satisfaction is difficult to

Wrap your beautiful mind around.

Your only response is to cry

Because that is the first skill you learned.

It hurts.

You take it like a woman

Because you are fourteen now

And expecting—

Expecting more from life.

Expecting a life.

A new life.

A newborn,

Who will cry

At its first breath

Just as you did.

You cry

Just as your mother did

When she gave life to you.

Motherhood

I am the purple orchids.

You are the root

Of the stem of the branches

Of the leaves.

You are the glue

That holds the crazy in me.

I was pieces

Until you put them together.

Fix

Body sounds.

Chest rising.

Shallow breathing.

Gurgling stomachs.

Gulping throats.

Closed eyelids.

Pupils sliding.

Limbs shifting.

Hearts beating.

Your body sounds

Are music to my soul

When I am next to you.

Connecting

The space in space is still forming.

You are still forming.

The universe is not complete.

The planets are shifting.

Stars are breaking constantly.

Suns bursting.

Heatwaves on heatwaves.

Sun gives life

To the earth.

You give life

To the future.

You are full of life

In all forms.

Worthy

The sun is out today

Yet there are those that live in the darkness.

Like the sun that glows on your face—

How do you plan on bringing light in those that live in the dark?

Will you be a shadow and give them shade?

Or will you be the sun and radiate?

Shade

Are the veins in your hand

Deep enough

For all the meeting points—

Each time you were not able to express yourself?

There is passion swirling inside you.

Thick

Human—
Let's be encouragers.
The world needs
A LOT
More love.

More

There is something beautiful about the way the rain falls.
There is something hurting about the way your tears fall.
Oceans deep with waves.
She feels.

Emotions

12-week-old fetus,
With a string-thin umbilical cord
Attached to your pink flesh.
Webbed fingers forming,
Ears seeking your mother's voice,
Eyes longing to see your mother's face,
Mouth shut permanently.
Your mother will never hear you cry,
And your heart will never beat
To live seconds worth of life.
You are flesh,
They told your mother.

Demise

A kind friend once told me—
Do not feel bad about feeling
Your feelings.
If you are hurt,
That just reminds you of the type of person
You do not need to be.
You hold hearts
As if they are glass in your palms.
The glass breaks.
It shatters.
People scatter.
But along the way
You come to know there is something out there
That is greater.
Along the way you come to understand
That everything
Will be okay.

Happiness of the Heart

FREED

Little Hugs

Raman places her poems in the centre of the page to bring her readers back to their centres. This creates balance on each page. Each poem contains an underlying theme. The title ends the poem to tie in the core concepts. Her poems are in no specific order. They are shuffled, as she wants to maintain the element of surprise and display that life events are not always in order.

For more little hugs
Social Media: littlehugsfromraman
Email: ramandeepmanderpoetry@gmail.com

Be love!
glow

♡

CPSIA information can be obtained
at www.ICGtesting.com
Printed in the USA
LVHW072342131019
633983LV00002BA/2/P